To

_____

From

_____

Date

_____

"A mother is she who can
take the place of all others
but whose place
no one else can take."
—Cardinal Mermillod

A Gift Book for Moms
and Those Who Wish to Celebrate Them

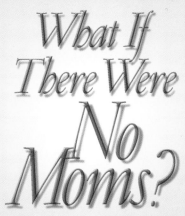

What If There Were No Moms?

HOWARD BOOKS
A DIVISION OF SIMON & SCHUSTER
New York   London   Toronto   Sydney

Caron Chandler Loveless
Illustrations by Dennis Hill

What if there were no moms? Really. Nowhere.
Like, what if one day they just *were not there*?

No notes on the fridges.

No voice mail.

No traces.

No moms in their normal,

predictable places.

We would fidget and fumble and bumble around,
at the thought that no mothers
might ever be found.

We'd worry, of course;
to police stations we'd go.
Report just the facts, what little we know!

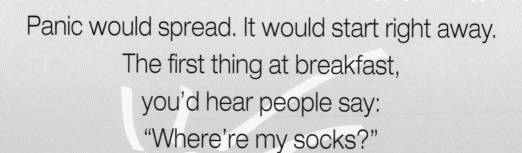

Panic would spread. It would start right away.
The first thing at breakfast,
you'd hear people say:
"Where're my socks?"

"Where's my homework?"
"I can't find the keys!"
"We're all out of milk!"
"I need my mom, please!"

Buses would bulge, chock-full of new riders.
With all mothers gone,
we'd lose our best drivers.

In this state of things there'd be
glitches galore,
matted hair in the sinks and crud on the floor.

Handwritten notes
would be things of the past.
"How was your day?"
Well . . . no one would ask.

The fridge would be bare on the outside and in,
no fruit drinks or ice cream
to share with a friend.

And when you're home sick,
no mom would appear
with a cool cloth
or soup
or a listening ear.

Who would take pictures
to mark your first date?
Then wait up and worry
when you come in late?

Forget family vacations
and summertime fun,
and that warning from Mom:
"Stay out of the sun!"

A kiss you would miss at the end of the day,
when your cheeks were on fire
'cause you didn't obey.

Who would clip coupons
or think to wash sheets,
or say, "Tell them thank you,"
and "Don't ever cheat"?

"There's a spot on your coat.
Here, I have just the thing."
Or "It's time
for the anthem.
Let's all stand
and sing."

The world would be dim,
minus candles and glitter.
With all mothers gone,
every cake would taste bitter.

Encouraging "mom" words
would never be spoken,
the perfect solution for hearts that are broken.

Lifesaving questions would seldom get asked:
"Did you wear your seat belt?"
"Does he drive too fast?"

Who would stand up as your number one fan,
telling the world you're the *best in the land*?

And what about birthdays?
Who'd buy the balloons?
Or sing "Happy Birthday"
a tad out of tune?

If moms all went missing,
our homes would be bare.
No paint on the wall,
not even a chair.

A gasp at a sunset would rarely take place,
with no mom to tell you
to slow down your pace.

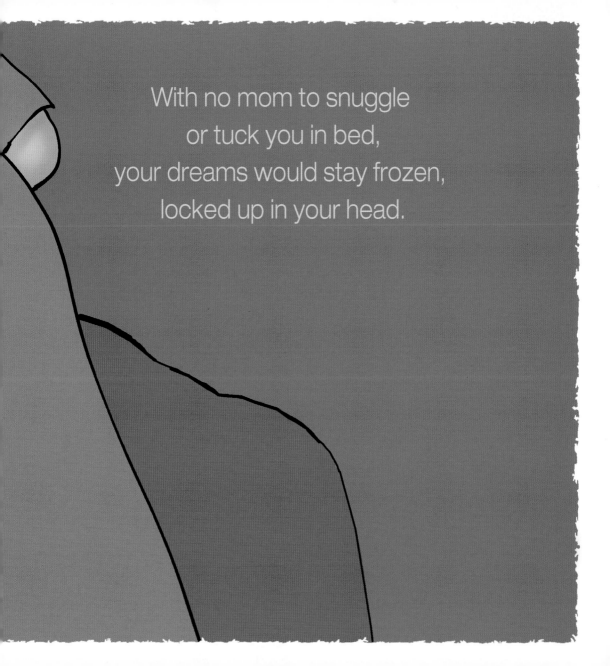

With no mom to snuggle
or tuck you in bed,
your dreams would stay frozen,
locked up in your head.

Without Mom,
no one would tell you
your family tree.
Who looks like you and
who looks like me?

So let's stop all this horror,
this folly, this fiction,
and celebrate Mom
with a jig in the kitchen!

Let's toss up the dish towels
and send out a cheer!
Tell Mom we miss her
when she isn't near.

Let's tell her we need her,
we cherish her presence.
Let's talk up her good points,
her beauty, her essence.

So to you, Mom,
I just have to say...

Could I live
without you?

Mom, I couldn't live without you because:

_____

_____

_____

_____

_____

_____

_____

_____

_____

_____

She takes good care of her family
and is never lazy. Her children will praise her.
—Proverbs 31:27–28a

Our purpose at Howard Books is to:
• *Increase faith* in the hearts of growing Christians
• *Inspire holiness* in the lives of believers
• *Instill hope* in the hearts of struggling people everywhere
Because He's coming again!

Published by Howard Books, a division of Simon & Schuster, Inc.
1230 Avenue of the Americas, New York, NY 10020
www.howardpublishing.com

What If There Were No Moms? © 2008 by Caron Chandler Loveless

Library of Congress Cataloging-in-Publication Data

Loveless, Caron, 1955-
  What if there were no moms / Caron Loveless ; illustrated by Dennis Hill.
    p. cm.
  1. Mothers—Poetry. 2. Christian poetry. I. Hill, Dennis. II. Title.
  PS3612.O838W47 2007
  811'.6—dc22
                         2007033648
ISBN-13: 978-1-4165-4225-4
ISBN-10:   1-4165-4225-6
10 9 8 7 6 5 4 3 2 1

Manufactured in China

For information regarding special discounts for bulk purchases, please contact: Simon & Schuster Special Sales at 1-800-456-6798 or business@simonandschuster.com.

Edited by Chrys Howard
Cover design by Stephanie D. Walker
Interior design by Dennis Hill and Stephanie D. Walker
Illustrations by Dennis Hill

Scripture quotations, unless otherwise marked, are from the Contemporary English Version, copyright © 1995 by American Bible Society. Used by permission.